Love and the Weather

Susan Gardner

For Jay White —
Susan Gardner
,5 April 2023

Susan Gardner is a poet and visual artist. She is the author of
seven books and has appeared in numerous anthologies. She
delivered the Cam Memorial Lecture at the New York Public
Library, where she was honored to be granted a year in the Allen
Room. She has presented extensive lectures and readings
including at the Freer Gallery of the Smithsonian Institution, the
Library of Congress, and the Folger Library. She has been invited
to residencies at the American Academy in Rome and many others
in interesting places, and her art has been exhibited internationally
in museums and galleries.   www.susangardner.org

Love and the Weather
Lifted to the Wind ~ Poems 1974~2015
To Inhabit the Felt World
Drawing the Line ~ A Passionate Life
Box of Light ~ Caja de Luz
Stone Music
Intimate Landscapes

Nightwork

In the night silence

the house hums darkly

wood creaks with memory of its tree life

refrigerator defrosts itself around ice cream

some small invisible creature scratches at the screen,

curls against the still warm wall

soft snores, shifting sheets

unseen stars

everyone sleeps in the dark

over the page

one bulb burns

word after word, one sheet after another.

At Hudson Bayou

On the edge of the bayou, I wait.

Now and then sounds break the silence—
egrets and pelicans dive through air
water laps at mangrove roots
mullets leap, splash wet silver shine.

Families of shy manatees
show themselves alongside the boat slip,
     gently churn the current,
     touch faces softly,
     nudge and guide the young.

Adolescent manatees the size of our dining table,
adults like smallish, mottled gray-brown whales,
snub, wrinkled noses
round, dark eyes under hoods of gray eyelids

tails— lobed fans my arm's length across the stern—

    wave slowly,

      propel these bayou giants

      to dare approach the boat slip

and—

      three feet apart —

share a silent gaze.

Drizzled Dawn

a fret of rain rouses the drizzled day

mist shimmers, passes, wheels back

until for a quarter hour it lifts

to reveal the edges of clouds

On St. Mullins' stone belfry walls above the river,

condominium-ed nests crowd higher,

in flapping air noisy thousands bank, curl,

shift to starboard, circle furiously

moot meeting of the parliament of crows

Locked Gate

On December 19, 1980
Alaíde Foppa went to buy flowers.
She disappeared.

Sixty-six years old.
In a cellar, in a bloody cell, in Guatemala,
by the hands of thugs.
Or worse.

I walk by Alaíde's sweet house in Tepoztlán,
refuge from city noise and endless sorrow
     Mario, husband of decades, killed
        in Guatemala by a car
    two sons, Mario and Juan Pablo,
         Guatemalan guerillas, dead
         Silvia, belovéd hija, hiding in Cuba
         Laura and Julio, safe
    in an unquiet life in Mexico.

Alaíde's house is closed.

White cotton curtains cross the fastened windows,

        embroidered flowers near the sills.

Past the locked iron gate, leaves blow in corners

        of the patio, brown on the stones,

        undisturbed.

Now and then, someone, thinking of Alaíde, tosses

        a message through the patterned bars,

        also undisturbed.

Thirty years ago, I write a poem, lift it to the wind,

        through the barred gate.

        Dust now.

Alaíde loved the light of Italian art

        and the music of Italian words.

Teacher, translator, scholar,

    for almost half a century, she put words on paper

        justice equality honor
           despair hope

No body. No grave. Not a strand of hair.

Only paper reminds us

    of her beauty, her courage

but a century after she was born, her words,

    written down,

    are read.

Remembered, like Joe Hill, she's alive as you or me.

At St. Canice's Cathedral, Kilkenny, Ireland

On the funerary cover, drapery
>shines black and beautiful,
centuries of parishioners have yielded to its tactile seduction
and left a polished ghost of their passing caresses.

Flesh and bones consumed by decades ticking on,
>century yielding to millennia,
and none of these lords and their few ladies
noticing at all.

My hand trails the looping folds of medieval Irish limestone,
>polished perfect black,
a shade thinner, more black now
than before I came.

And I, too, am a shade thinner,
a microscopic layer of fingertips left on this lady's robe
cloaks her eternity,
not mine yet.

Riverhead

Born in cloud

a rivulet rolls down the top of the watershed

falls into its course

moves each pebble, each minima of silt,

pushes topsoil and boulders captured

in the dams of beavers and humans

tumbles again white and rapid over rocky flumes,

murky as it spawns new oxbows,

lethargically clears old floodplains,

every inch unreplicated,

every moment passed is past.

Gone.

At the last, every roiled dram

joins the sea,

born again to cloud.

Summer Idyll

one note from a child's flute

resting on the air

like a swallow on the porch rail

summer dusk glimmers

nightbird serenades the moon

your voice remembered

Tea

sage tea

steam drifting transparently

      slowly... slowly...

releases its fragrance

soft golden green

held by a shred of burned earth

perfumes of hillsides and sunrise

the bitter-clean taste of morning

holding sunlight forever

in tiny black bits

whispering in the darkness

longing to set free the golden being

it has been from the beginning

Slow Wind Wallow Redux

June 2011 538,049 acres of Arizona and New Mexico
                              burning.
June 2012 update 289,000 acres of New Mexico burning.
June 2021 update 2,569,009 acres of California burning.
June 2022 update 899,453 acres of New Mexico burning.
July 2022 update 2,002,408 acres burning now.

Burning. Burning up. Burning down.
Biologists cross the fire line, corral electro-stunned
Gila trout.
Fish to spend summer vacation in northern New Mexico.

Dark smoke clouds stutter by
snag on rocky crags
fall in the cooling night air

smoke rains into our forest, our town, our skin
smoky glare fills Sunday morning
murky air too heavy to drift away

microbits of everywhere

in our eyes

in our lungs

with us now and forever

until we also are

microbits.

*National Oceanic and Atmospheric Administration fire information

Inheritance

ruddy sky burdens serrated city canyons
street arroyos run with exhaust-ed rivers

over nearby sea, west wind
wrenches up curls of oily particulate inheritance

    scorched primeval forests surge in the frenzied air
    plumes of mud-wracked plankton

    undeciphered primeval forests,
    inchoate volatile haze of our past

    liquid dinosaurs, antediluvians, homo habilis, return
    stratus clouds of forgotten faces

before dusk, green sky cold as lead—
sometime arrives

Ghost Along the Tracks

Rough-cut stones ragged in roofless granite walls,

piled up, heaped on what was once the floor.

Where windows were,

perfect rectangles of the mason's craft look in.

The room once low-roofed, dark, enclosed,

now illuminated by refractive rolling mist.

Every standing stone silvered in waves,

amidst the grasses, lupines, wild barley,

nourished by grounded clouds,

the rosy blooming rowan-ash reclaims its place.

Forbearance

through this long showery day

clouds scud in the wind

chase isobars of cold air

across the roiling jet stream

spring arrives in freezing sunshine

stutters

backslides

bows in on the back of cold April bluster

frost traces each greening leaf

snug nestlings keep in sheltering aeries

peony buds close back on themselves

tomato blossoms explode in icy dismay

riven with desire

all wait for another day

Night Table

I

Dusk eases past the horizon
 dark sky shines
 traces high-piled clouds

Beside the bed
 essentials crowd the night table
  clock radio lamp
  novel eyeglasses

 breath of spring garden
  small pitcher with a sprig of lilac
  panicles' drowsy eyelids
  already drooping

 pencil next to the leather notebook
  scent of trees
  whiff of the life they once had
  waiting for a new life of words

tea in a china cup without a saucer

scents of spices

faraway hills

journeys and dreams

photograph

remembrance of a sweet day

aspens glowing

your smile alight

II

dusk has its way

night draws each body

over the moonless horizon

orbiting toward dawn

Jupiter rises

dazzles the stars

24

III

sleep is temporary death.

a few things
awaken us to this life

Marriage

I That Day

Knock your elbow against the edge of the door
the funny bone sends a thrill of shock
right to our brain.

On this hot morning
our eyes knock.

    every bone funny
    every muscle laughing
    every hair breathless

In the aftershock we keep touching
that electric pain
lean against the doorframe
until our hearts can move again.

II Whiteout

All night we lie

under our white comforter

in the comfort of our white bed

while the snow slides over the mountain

and lies down over everything

In the morning feeble sun

glimmers down

until the cloud-blanket evaporates

in great sheets of silence

III Apoptosis

shed cells

ambition

sorrow

keep joy

little by little

grow old with me

Waiting

in dark stillness

against night clouds, city lights

light your sleeping face

waiting for the morning

and your sleepy smile

so inaccessible

until sleep

ruptured by consciousness

desires the day

Old Enough

Being productive makes a person
very busy.

I was imagining idleness
but it turns out to be a daydream.

We are going to be old pretty soon.
We have been very busy but pretty soon
we will be old enough
to dream.

Kiss me now and make a plan
to kiss me again
pretty soon
when we are old enough.

The time is now.

Black Tea

black tea in a mug

over the rim

my sore heart's dearest friend

smiles old love at me

Overnight

clouds swollen black against blacker hills

scraps of pewter sky crack out

over ground dark with icy rigidity

hoar sky gleams low

traces of fog glitter

rimed with chill damp

over serrated summits, no reflection

only pale flat gray

 a cloud-veiled snowless day

fireplace burns last year's piñon

at the window, first silent snow

threatens already fat lilac buds

virgin blue to shriveled brown

in the moonlit frost, fleeting fertility

lost to April inconstancy

Garden Bench

Narrowing path

    overrun with elephant ears, birds-of-paradise,

    pampas grass, plumed with decay,

Relentlessly accelerates. Tentacles avid,

    sumptuous excess traces slow wind,

    in trees' canopy, leaves reach for sky.

Late sun glints through heavy foliage,

    silence and noise, garden leaves,

    insects and wind, muffled footsteps.

Between seasons, on gray schist legs

    angled apart

    the stone rests.

Each dry winter, cemented

    in their shrunken rigid waterless bed

    desiccated stems flake to dust.

Leaves of streamside trees

    wait for July rain

    to decompose.

Each rainy summer night stone sinks another iota

    toward its ancestral home amidst the bedrock

        the river's underground channel

        tipping imperceptibly aslant

        in the slippery loam.

The path a dirt track, no longer wide enough for two people

    to pass, once planted, now wild.

Below steep rock steps, a derelict fountain,

    verdigris-bronze head on the wall,

    calcified mouth unable to spout the rainy runoff.

There the bench waited for decades.

A stone in the river, washed smooth

    in its muddy bed, wet in the sunshine,

its solid actuality contains

    the igneous history of the world.

Friends drink coffee

sun warms the humid morning

with the edge of her hand

one sweeps a wavy hair from her ear

walking on the road

eyes touch

hands reach for sky

a bell is sounding

against the hill

too far away to hear

at dusk, in the last light

we wait

aroused by the coming night air

Politics of the Body

My heart, a little left of center,

contracts and pumps

five hundred times an hour

tucked in behind a thin cage

tough lungs push and retreat

a thousand times an hour

all to send a bottle's worth of oxygen

around the network, pass by the brain,

brushing each molecule just enough

for love math art rage despair poems hope

just enough for one life for one hour—

better living through chemistry.

Summer Twilight

in the darkening hour, the meadow alight with rising moon,

cicadas flitter in hurried, desperate lust

invisible grass touched only by dew

a girl stops a moment

listens to shadows

Deep Water

sun-stunned dark water
defines curved blue atmosphere
ultramarine horizon invisible

skin flames in fevered summer air
sweat a salty sheen,
curls a frizzy nimbus over reddening ears

legs stiff at water's boundary
plunge in, drown in brilliant delight
weightless, jubilant

float besotted

I learn to swim

Leftovers

sycamore leaves big as my face

fall all over themselves

yellow ochre, umber,

last traces of red in the veins

summer's green still at the edges

a tweed carpet of leftovers

on the grounded slopes

December Ghost

sun shines silent on tattered rime
morning ice glimmers
sap is still this brilliant day

snow-weighted juniper trees
grayed fence posts askew
shadows across iced fields

one withered white rose tethered lightly
on a long trailing old cane
last ghost of summer

One and Only

Veil of fat cirrus,

filled with pebble-shards of ice,

condenses in the frigid high air

freezes around earthly molecules,

wind-whirled, dissolves, freezes again,

coalesces into a hexagon.

Falling crystal, shaped by wind, cold,

neighboring adolescent crystals, droplets,

descent through spiraling atmosphere,

the multitude of snowflakes

passes through sharp air,

comes to rest in the river,

each the perfect image of its life story,

all precisely aligned in their brief eternity

alike in their exceptionality.

Rocky Mountain Dusk

at 20,000 feet slow-blown virga wavers
frozen virgin veils shyly fall away
to a higher stronghold

black clouds scud over less black mountains
longed for snow
fractures winter rainbow

Multimedia

Does god fit in your box?

Did you hear a voice from your television say,

> I am here

Did your computer take you to a website and say,

> You are here

Did you see the billboards along the highway,

> The end is near.

> All can be saved.

> Repent!

Each of us will try not to see

our own demon

but someday,

perhaps accidentally,

we will look in the mirror.

Partita

I   Coffee break

they lean into the space between them
faces illuminated with interest
or pheromones
they leave their coffee to grow cold

he explains

       the phenomenological world

       materialist dialectics

       Kama sutra

blind to the world
they take one breath,
exhale,
then one more

deaf to all but one voice,
bellies, breasts, crotch, hair,

focused,

limerance absolute

immeasurable, preposterous, unquenchable appetite

ravenous for bone and skin

avid for muscle, fat, blood

finger pads on webbing of toes

hair against breast, tongue edging earlobe

voice in the valley

notched between the ends of clavicles

the roar of alive

II   Wilderness

proud possessor of toes and taste buds

deaf director of board and bed

anxious hoarder of stuff no one wants

he craves more

she holds hurt in her bones

in mind, in dreams

at the edge of fingernails

scraping the soul

two, cancered with regret,

calloused with unanswered forgiveness

shrunk into a teaspoon of sown salt.

III   Weight

Hard tumor of hurt.

How great the need

for absolution.

Unrequited, untouched

by contrition or amends

breathless weight

thick in outstretched arms

fingers bent backward

under its pitiless mass.

The heart must heal itself.

Breath of Mercy

Hard edged cold slides in

ribs rigid, pleural sacs hold iced shards of air

lungs freeze from inside out

white fingernails roll over

round reddened fingers

on fire with cold

burning cold runs through each phalanx of fingers and toes

lodges in stiff knuckles immovable

in frozen jackets of useless ligaments

Rime of sleep wraps tight, eyelids droop

sparkles of crimson, cobalt, citrine

warm the last slivers of fading, euphoric mind

Folded fog

at Haein-sa (Temple of the Ocean Mudra), Korea

wind swirls from the mountains
    leaves quiver hazard the rain

surreptitious fog slides in
    skims over the folded hills

obscured in somber dusk
    amorphous mist coils through engulfing torrents

under hidden moonlight
    fleeting deluge whelms the canopy

water laps across flat stones
    riffles betray muted cloud shine

in the dim gloaming   somewhere near
    a song

Eye on the Storm

on the edge of a tumbling storm

dark sky, ruffled fronds, shifting bay

birds fold in on themselves

everyone tucked in

jumping at the chance

to go out in the pauses

between rain waves until

another wind-driven surge spills over everything

War Game Redux

I They All Say So

All of them,
  Romans, Goths, Visigoths
  Saxons, Anglos, Vikings
  Persians and Medes
  Vedas and Mongols
  Hans and Xings

On and on
They all say

  "Mine is bigger than yours "

Presbyterian Hindus
  Buddhist Catholics
  Zoroastrian Jews
  Taoist Realist Idealists

On and on

They all say

"Mine is bigger than yours "

SO?

II Unsettled Conditions

Sun tomorrow

followed by cloudy days

then rain

Breezy conditions

small craft warnings

large lakes advisory

turbulence in the upper atmosphere

Any time is the time

to go to war.

III Fever

Hot faces

Hot words

Fever of hate

Fire in the blood

Shoot hack rip rape

Slash burn bomb

What else can you do?

What else can we do?

talk of honor

talk of sacrifice

talk of harm's way

then shoot.

Desperate want

To wake you at dawn,

      hands aflame, tongue fervent,

      skin blood burnished

      slake morning thirst with your sweet sweat

      scrawl my desires on your skin

      write my name on your mind

      lips still, tongue fat, ears cold

      body hungers.

I want to stay for a little while longer

      evade the desolation of your absence

      evoke your ghost

      assuage my scorched spirit

for a little while longer

I wanted to evade the grief

that like a great, free eagle

soars through my heart

Passage

shards of bone, eyelashes,

    white wool sweater,

no struggle, one soft gasp, one more

    eyes open, he tastes his last air

smashed body shudders still

    life-light pours out into cold air

all that is needed to leave this life

    radiates away

beneath the elderberry unstill hearts

    sink with him

Red Net

flushed air flat in the heat

the weight of this afternoon

immobile

in its net of red light

late sun has captured the world whole

Change of Season

Waterfall falling

running down the cheeks of the hills.

Spring rain tumbles

in the cleft of the rock.

Air sprays of icy fragrance

tears blown over the impenetrable sky.

Recollected

Your voice reminds me

      after so long a time

how sweet our days

I love the memory of loving you.

Dearest friend, I love you still

Granada, October

sunlight chases

whirling yellow chestnut leaf —

a tizzy of shine

rain runs under stones

chills the ripening garden

pleats the evening air

wind rises

maple leaf blazes through dusky air

ricochets through first snow

Held Close

In the kindly embrace of close-held love
the touch of familiar affection
fills my heart.

Our faces suffuse with a blush of surprise
in the pleasure of our company.

Not One Eighth

Not one eighth of a millimeter

space enough

     unbounded

     extravagant

     uncontested

     unconditional

   for prairies of quarks and muons

   to find themselves locked in atomic

   attachment

Not one eighth of an inch from you,

I am

     profligate

     spendthrift

     improvident

     imprudent

enough to fill galactic silences, shriek strings

across the frozen black topography

to grace the electrons of our nucleus

locked in immortal attachment

Physics of the Iris

*Iris, courier of the gods, travels her rainbow to
carry messages between heaven and earth*

The body of one

    rages with joy

against the surface of the other

struck by lightning

dazzled

dazed

in a sidereal cloud, as apart

as infrared and ultraviolet

as hydrogen and oxygen

the spectrum broken open

electric songs resounding

in thundering air

in a delirium of molecules let loose

the critical mass

achieved

Iris flying home

with old news

Sticks and Stones

Once upon a time, I saw a line. I saw the paper pull the ink from the brush and the brush, one hair at a time, relinquish the ink, allowing it to become a line, to settle into its destiny.

Stone terrain
blue-black obsidian stage waiting
round water beads shine with expectation

clinging smell of charred carbon powder and glue
loops over the surface
rumors of friction wearing at stick and stone

water droplets blacken,
marble over anthracite well of the grinding stone
formless, boundless lake of blackness spreads

time lengthens
ink carried on wavy sheep's hair
pulled into paper

becomes poem, book, pine branch painting

letter of good-bye

stain on the table

inadvertent turnings bleed at the edges

thickness of the line varies by pressure applied

onto each felted fiber

brush relinquishes its charge,

sets free the ink it carries

to inhabit the felt world.

Cézanne's Apples

Eye-shape bowl

    ringed dark around the iris

    periphery between color and air

Suspended within the apparent ivory black

    flat black bands concentrate roundness

    border between light and no light

Palette heavy with odors of trees, sweet seeds, acrid

solvents

Prussian blue   wanting red, Swiss Diesbach made sky

Paris blue   Paris green, French revolution

Hooker's green   for perfect English leaves

Payne's gray   less black than black, precise tints

    seep through leaking light

Vermeer blue   precious pure ultramarine,

    lapis lazuli from Badakhshan,

    blooming with lead and wars

Orchestrated chemistry

cochineal, carmine stain of fugitive insects

cinnabar, slippery mercury

citrine, golden light of ground gems,

gamboge, resin for sunlight, monks' robes

cobalt cerulean indigo viridian

umber, the smell of Italy's hillsides

sienna, Tuscany's earth, moved to galleries

lead, life to colors, death to artists

paint linen geometry

Eyes open to the world as it may be

Acknowledgements

I thank the authors who have entrusted their work to me for expanding my literary universe and for the friendship that came through poetry. For their reading of early drafts and encouragement, I thank Donald Platt, Irena Praitis and Sylvia Byrne Pollack, and for kind words, thank you to poet-friends Jay White, Steven Cramer, Mary Gilliland and Marvel Harrison.

Once again, RD has insisted that poetry is part of our life. The books would not be out in the world without him.

Some of the poems in this volume have appeared elsewhere in altered form, just like our lives through the last few years. A few have been in reviews, in various anthologies, or in my previous books, deeply changed as I reconsidered some familiar themes.

"Locked Gate" appeared in plume #9, spring 2021.

ISBN 978-1-952204-14-2
Printed in the United States of America

Love and the Weather is set in Avenir, a geometric font based on
the circle, designed by Adrian Frutiger in 1987, released in 1988
by Linotype GmbH.

RED MOUNTAIN PRESS

Bainbridge Island, Washington
www.redmountainpress.us